# A PEBBLE, WASHED ASHORE

*By*

Mariet van Knippenberg

Cyberwit.net
4/2 B, L.I.G.
Govindpur Colony,
Allahabad-211004 (U.P.)
India

Tel: 91-532-2541153
E-mail: cyberwit@rediffmail.com
www.cyberwit.net

**A PEBBLE, WASHED ASHORE**

Mariet van Knippenberg



ISBN 81-8253-012-1
First Edition : June 2004
Rs. 150/-

Typeset by Vaishnavi Enterprises, Kamla Nagar, Allahabad
Printed in India at Astha Associates, D. N. Marg, Allahabad

# THE AUTHOR

Mariet van Knippenberg was born on December 5th 1953 in a little town called Kessel in the south of the Netherlands. "Coming from a very musical family, I found out at early age that I love music and words put to it. At school, languages were among my favourites classes and I speak besides Dutch and Limburgs, the language spoken in my area also German and English and some French. In the time I worked and got married I didn't have much time to do something with words, being busy with raising two wonderful sons Rob, 25 now and Frank, 22. Not till after I discovered the internet, chat rooms and boards I found out that I am kinda addicted to what words can express. After a close friend wrote a poem about my nickname *pebble* and another friend encouraged me to try myself I wrote my first poem...Pillow Talk...which got an award right away and was published. And then I just couldn't stop, there were days when I wrote 5 poems a day. Last year October I started writing lyrics for songs too and so far very successful, I have 8 contracts so far with a music publisher and cant wait to hear them being recorded. My family and friends supported me all the time, my sister and brothers never got tired reading my poems and being positive and the same goes for Lauri.. my ex-husband and best friend. At the moment, I am divorced and I am living with my boys. Poetry helped me through some bad times, like you can read in my poems, a divorce, the death of my father and a painful ended relationship. A dream will come true with this book and I hope that I can write much more."

# DEDICATION

To my father Harry van Knippenberg who always believed in me and who died December 9th 2002, to my family and to Mario.

# CONTENTS

# PEBBLES

Like a pebble is washed ashore
i will come into your life
maybe I will move on fast
maybe I will stay a while
and rest and listen to your story
and tell you mine
time will tell

# I WAS A PEBBLE, WASHED ASHORE

Okay, you can throw me back now
as far as you can
don`t mind me ever coming back
just sinking to the bottom
of an endless ocean
where the burning sun
never reaches the silver sand
and the cool moonlight
is as far as the stars are
where no coral, no nothing grows
only blind fish will accompany me
and I will lie down in pain and anger
there I will rest
till another huge wave
will pick me up again
and washes me to a new shore
but it will never be
your shore again

## GRAINS OF SAND BETWEEN MY TOES

I follow footsteps in the sand
two big feet
and little ones, from a dog
just me, the sea
and above that all
like a giant roof
the deep blue sky
sometimes
I bend over
to pick up a shell
blue and white
tender like china
I try to step into
those big traces
trying to leave the sand
untouched, just perfect
a memorial
for all the shells
that were crushed on this shore
all the jelly fish
that ended their lives
washed upon against their will
all the pebbles
that are waiting to be picked
so I just walk along
following the footsteps

# DREAMS IN SAND

Wake up, little pebble
its about time
you start living again
dreams are nice
but dreams are made
of sandman's dust
and one day
all the dust he used
will be blown
in those big blue eyes
and they will start
to burn
from tears, never cried
over lost friendship
and lost love
that wasn't meant to be
sandman saw
before you did
he can be mean
an old man, looking for victims
innocent, naive ones
who fall into mean traps
the old man sets for them
laughing over pain and sorrow
so wake up, little pebble
before the weight of time
crushes you
leaving nothing
but the dust of time

# EYES WIDE OPEN

Sand, white sand
as far as my eyes can see
burning white
hurting my eyes
so I close them
I lie there
letting the sand
warm my body
being rocked asleep
by the sound, the love song
of the endless breakers
of the ocean
that seems to be you
you come to me
in coloured waves
blue as the sky
and green as the mysterious depth
of cool underwater landscapes
you pick me up
and let me ride on that wave
till I break down
and land on my own shore again
not crushed, not broken
but more whole
than I ever was before

## SEVENTEEN

I was seventeen once
and full of dreams
I was looking for a wonder
stars and silver beams
princes filled my fantasies
knights in armors bright
when would they come to pick me up
when would they start the fight
with bad guys and with dragons
that would spread only fear
a virgin, tied and shivering
who wept and spilled her tears

How blue I was at seventeen
romantic to the bone
I blushed, when someone looked at me
I panicked when he phoned
the bad world was outside
and I better stayed in
the good girls would be rescued and
my knight would surely win
not only fighting dragons
but also my pure heart
and then he would take me home
and we would never part

How innocent can a girl be
how long can she wait
for true and everlasting love
that`s made in heavens gate
A virgin and an angel child
that no harm could touch
until she found that princes

and knights you have to watch
for they can be the dragons too
the bad guys in disguise
and at the end the darkest knight
takes them to paradise

# KESSEL

How proud my little town is
on the borders of the river
it's castle, or what's left of it
rising high above the houses
the church and it's mighty tower
dominate the view
next to it the cemetery
where my father rest

How beautiful my little town is
with its market place
where the old man
is resting on a bench in the sun
and the ancient houses
watch the slow traffic
passing my
time means nothing to them

How grateful for this little town, I am
born and raised in it
it still attracts me, calls me home
how I want to live there
feel it's embrace, it's care
I left it, years ago
but it never left me
and one day, I will go home

# MEMORIES

They say, she tells me
that the man on the painting
the one, hanging on the wall
was my husband
long ago
but I don‘t believe them
and she looks at me
with eyes, that ask
who are you anyway
and I wonder
will I ever forget
the way you look
the way I feel
the way we love
will I be
like this little lady
will i ever look
at my grandchild
with the same empty blue eyes
And I can only pray

# THREE JELLIES FOR A DIME

A little store
not more place then a living room
in the old fashioned days
in it, shells
filled with cigars, matches
paper and pens
and candy, lots of candy
outside
the dark church
it's tower throws a shadow
on the little town on the river
inside its cosy, warm
a little boy
he cannot keep his eyes
off all the candy he sees
under the glass
hidden from warm children's hands
he thinks long
the lady is waiting
what to pick? what is the best
his finger hesitates
the lady smiles and asks
do you know , what it will be
little William
he sighs and says
with a soft wondering voice
I want it all
and she just nods
cause she understands him so well

# FREEDOM HAS IT'S PRICE

A little red balloon
on a yellow rope
tied to a little boys arm
is trying to get free
so much is it longing
to fly away
to see the world
from high above
up with the birds
up with the kites
fly away to the sun
little does it know
about dangers
about winds and storms
little does it know
about rain and snow
it only sees the light up there
a little red balloon
desperate
trying to escape
and looking at it
I want to fly along

# PIETA

The serenity
on her face
touches me deep
in her snow white arms
the dead body
of her tortured son
blood of her blood
Carefully
she wipes away
the spilled drops
caressing
his wounded face and body
where the executioner
did his dirty job
hurting
for pleasure
killing
for the kick
leaving her
with the remains
of the one
she loved above all
and hiding her tears
she gives in
to the knowledge
that this was meant to be

# ARABIAN NIGHTS

The mystery
of a desert moon
her rays of soft light
drawing strange figures
on the waves
of an endless sea of sand
inside the blinded tent
a melancholic sound
of a magic flute
a dark goddess
dancing slowly
her tempting hips
move in circles
and the transparent veils
play a game of colours
men, not even noticing, it seems
this dream of desires
sip their hot mocha
and talk, argue about
what men, who can have it all
interests most
weapons, fights
camels and horses
later on, the dancing girl
will follow another dance
without an audience
an ancient rhythm
to the beat of two hearts
just with who of them
she doesn`t know yet

# IF ONLY SHE HAD WAITED ONE MORE DAY

He saunters in
coming from outside
the hall seems cool
he looks around and his eyes catch her
she lies there, like thrown away
one hand on the floor
the other on her heart
she seems to smile
he runs to her, sighing
there you are my love, I looked everywhere
he takes her hand
its cold, like marble, stone
colder than anything, he touched before
what happened to her
Was it a disease, was it?
he sees men and women stumbling down streets
crying, yelling for help
death wondering around, looking for victims
the plague, nobody is free from
Was it murder, was it?
where is the knife, the string
where is the one, that took this lovely flower
and why, why her
she didn`t have anything worth stealing
only the gem, the jewel, she herself was
Was it a broken heart, was it?
the knowing she had to go on without him
without the loved one, so cold, so lonely
endless days to come
and not the courage to endure them
she waited so long for him

He will never know
All he wants is to sit with her
hold her hand, try to warm it with his breath
and remember how it could have been

# IF ONLY HE WOULD HAVE COME BACK ONE DAY EARLIER

Her longing for him
is so huge
much bigger than anything
she has ever felt before
she tries to get her mind set on other things
going out every day
trying to help the people
they are visited by the plague
that goes around in streets
and knocks on doors, unwelcome
by the ones that live there
frightened, to open the door
and give their children, their loved ones
to death, who comes to collect
and doesn`t look at age
she feels safe with sickness
she feels lost at home
frightened by every little sound
afraid of every noise she hears
her heart aches
and she thinks, he will never get back
is it worth dying for, this love
and she decides
yes , it is

# CHECKMATE

The wind blows liquid silver
and it covers the moon
in clouds of dust
I shiver
as my body
feels the cold breeze
surrounding it
with little iced needles
I stumble and fall
trying desperately
to reach the tower
in the middle of nowhere
like a ghost
focused on a beam of light
that calls me to it
promising a safe haven
a queen, robbed from her crown
chased by horses and knights
to win maybe at the end
more likely to lose
and when this is over
a new game will start
and I will be once again
at the mercy of the player

# REMEMBER THE FLYING MONKEYS

Familiar names whirling in my head
like a long yellow brick road
like forever twisting and turning
through a landscape.. so wide
with green and purple and honey
that keeps my poor heart yearning

Familiar feelings finding their way
into my nervous tummy
the sweet touch of little wings
a thousand busy butterflies
colourful beings dancing inside
making me wonder of what it brings

Familiar needs blowing my mind
singing in the sunshine together
with friends so very well known
as desire and longing and hoping
to accompany me on my journey
to refind my way back home

# WONDERLAND

Did you hear what happened
the country in distress
whispers in every corner
gone is the happiness

From servant up to farmer
from lady to the queens room
they all keep talking...talking
about this recent doom

The king on his mighty thrown there
his crown hanging over one ear
its no sight, I tell ya
they blame the jester, so I hear

But did that crown get larger
or did the royal head suddenly shrink
is it something the good witch could alter
with a magic spell or a wink

So jester, if you are guilty
be glad this is just a fairy tale
cause if this was the king and queen from Alice
you would lose your head ...that I can tell

# ERIC

Wasting in the bathroom
left there all alone
sits a rubber ducky
next to brush and comb
Giles, who is his owner
only needs him once a day
when he bathes and showers
rushing.. with no delay

Poor little Eric
what did he do to deserve
such a lonely life here
getting to his nerves
If only kids would be there
and play and fool around
dipping and splashing the water
dripping it on the ground

Little Eric sighing
dreaming his own wet dreams
of soap and hot bubbles
of gel and shaving cream

# TIME TO DO SOME SHOPPING

I am not that good
at making things with my hands
but now
I am gonna build
myself my dream guy
so lets see
his eyes
should be like yours
soft and loving
his lips
should kiss like yours
sweet and tender
his arms
should hold me like you hold me
during long cold nights
his heart
should beat for me
like I feel yours beat
when we are close
I wonder where to get
all those body parts

# ICELAND

Last night the ice queen
paid a visit to my bed
she must have come
in the one hour, that I could sleep
and this morning, early
I felt she took her share
of the warmth, my body lives on
she must have thought
she had every right to collect
what I am sure, is mine
and now my white skin
feels like frozen
my inside feels like iced
my head is spinning
and I have a feeling
I will never be warm again
if I start to cry
it wont be tears
rolling down my cheeks
it will be silver balls
little pearls of ice
making a tinkling sound
hitting the ground
and scatter into a million
in white ice crystals
all I want to do is sleep
sleep to forget
slumber away
into total forgetting of the world
like a puppet in a glacier
to be found in a far future

maybe I am just coming down with the flu

# SMOKE SIGNALS

He : sighs in despair
She : waits patiently

The wood is wet
it will not burn
he tried to light it all

She stares into the sky
no cloud in sight
she is waiting for his call

He : starts to smile
She : still waits

A little flame
finds its way
into the hill of wood

Her eyes are clear
a single tear
if only she understood

He : panics
She : laughs

A blanket on fire
a lot of smoke
he kept it all to close

She reads the smoke
and gets the message
too funny words he chose

# THE PATH

The path seems chosen
the choice is made
no need for me to hesitate
the thorns that come
with roses sweet
to fear the pain, there is no need
for all I see
is light ahead
all through the tunnel, traces set
where will it take me
I will understand
the moment, that you take my hand
and lead me through
I let myself go
and fear no fight
feel safe with you as my guide
to heal what was torn
and mend what was broken
with magic words, even unspoken
you lift me up
to dazzling height
above the clouds in the pure sunlight

# THE MOUNTAIN MAN

He fills his days
with walking the paths
that show his yesterdays trace
his goats they know
where he will lead
it is the same old place
as yesterday, or the day before
and as it will be tomorrow
they follow him blind
as he will protect
their days from harm and sorrow

He lives his life
far from the crowds
the cities that he hates
they abandoned him
left him no choice
he didn`t share their plates
what was served on them
he couldn`t chew
so he left far to the hills
who needs someone
they don`t really live
just eat, sleep and pay their bills

Here is his home
under that sky
of endless colourful blue
the sun at day
the moon at night
he knows his way is true
but sometimes the wind
catches him in the dark

and plays his wicked game
and deep in the caves
you can hear the sigh
as the echo repeats her name

For her, he went
without her no joy
the loneliness is his curse
the choice he made
was bitter and hard
but staying would have been worse
so he left all he had
all the goods worth a lot
all his family and friends
and he will stay here alone
alone with his beasts
until his lonely end

# THE HEAD IS STILL GOOD

My body is betraying me
after all these years
after all I did for it
all the care it got
I never counted
the hot showers it got
all that nice smelling soap
the creams, the lotions
to keep its skin
soft and tender
all the vitamins
A, all the B's
not to mention
the rest of the alphabet
I kept it cool in summer
with jumps in the pool
and gallons of water, I drank
I kept it from sunburns
and in wintertime
it was warm dressed
and nourished with the heat
of a open fire and a glass of wine
I kept it from rain and snow
from storm and lightning
My body is betraying me

I wonder where I could get a new one

# NEVER ON SALE

I am a seller
of dreams
wishes and thoughts
feelings, sad or happy
some are mine
some are yours
some are true
some will be one day
it's not a shop, I work in
nothing on the shelfs
you can order
but I never will promise
to deliver
and sometimes
even I
am out of stock

# FAREWELL

I look out on the land
around me only mist
I feel like I am
the only living person here
all the rest died
my hair, strains of moist curls
water is dripping on my coat
a sad day for my soul
a day I said goodbye
to my life, the life I knew
the fog is surrounding me
forming me into a shadow
it hides me
from eyes, I seem to see
predators, sneaking up to me
trying to eat my soul
screaming, go back
back to safety
security
before we come
crawl up on this hill
our paws wet from the grass
threatening
to eat you alive
I sigh and think of what lies ahead
You, a life together
I sigh again
Wave goodbye
And disappear in the mist

# OLD MILL ROAD

The sun goes down
and the last rays of sunlight
turn the deserted road
into a magical place
where shadows hide
the shapes of the houses
turning them into
soft edged lines
I look around
where am I ?
I know I was dreaming
but why am I here
are these someone else's memories
of a past
that I didn`t live
I know
I am searching
for someone, something
and that I am not afraid
and I know
I will be back here tomorrow
in the same dream

# BATTLE FOR LIFE

All your life
you are a soldier
in some way
always fighting
for your freedom
your body ready
for battles
fought out in hidden places
at night
fighting against
fears, known and unknown
dark forces
rejection
windmills, it seems
but what
if that fight ever ends
isn`t that
when life itself ends

# NO FALL IN MY HEART

I am sitting in my garden
and watch the tree
a leaf
gets my attention
it's hanging high
almost at the top
it has started to colour
the sun lightens up
its edges
gold and red
suddenly
the wind catches it
it shivers and starts to fall
tumbling down, turning, floating
it lies itself down
on a bed of other leaves
that fell before
and soon it will be covered
by hundreds
that will follow
the tree doesn't seem to care
it cut off
all those life bringing juices
and left the leaf to die
wish I could let go
that easy

# TIME IN A GLASS

You are like sand
slipping through my fingers
like I am watching
an hour glass
not able
to stop time
to stop events
from happening
is this destiny
finding
and giving up again
sometimes
I just want
to smash the glass
and run

# I JUST DID IT

I just smashed the glass
in which was kept
the sand of time
its running down
from the table
onto the floor
it's broken dreams
shattered hearts
it finds its way
into the narrow openings
in the wooden floor
lost for ages
all I can do
is pick up the pieces of glass
and go look for the vacuum cleaner

# DEFICIENCY

I juggle
with wrong and right
trying to keep
the perfect balance
right on the right
feeling so wrong sometimes
wrong on the left
the cursed side for things to happen
feeling right so much
and me in the middle
trying to keep
my eyes focused
on one of them
falling
sliding away
and then back to the other
my whole life will be like this
emotions - feelings
measuring all that happens
correcting the balance
with moves
some wise, some foolish
some so wrong
that things seems hopeless
all the way

# TOMORROW, I WILL TRY AGAIN

This day is empty
my whole world was empty
when I looked around
and saw
what a mess I made
what traces I left
in souls of friends
who believed me to be
dedicated and true
I am human
I can fail
and admitting failure
is maybe
the first step to forgiveness

# CHERRY BLOSSOM

Sunshine
and I saw
the first butterfly today
first one was yellow
like a lemon
flying around
soft wings
like covered
with soft powder
dancing in the spring air
from flower to flower
colours
that belong to spring
a festive yellow
blue, sky colours
a tender pink and white
is showing on trees
like a bride
wears her dress
so are the trees
dressed up
to celebrate
that winter is gone
and that the earth
has survived
another battle

# ROSEBUD

On a warm spring day
I discover the rose
a bud still
covered with dew
like a thousand
little vivid diamonds
glistening
in the rays of light
and from every day on
I admire it more
velvet red petals
promising
a magnificent summer
a wonderful smell

Then one day
I come and see
a broken stem
a hand came
and picked my flower
ripped it off
robbing me from its beauty
leaving me
with an empty feeling
of loss in my heart

# MY FLOWER

Green grass
as far as my eyes can see
daisies
like white with golden dots
look like
a gentle giant came around
and threw them
all around in circles
precious flowers
worth more in my world
than gold and diamonds
how can I ever explain
what my heart feels
when I look at them
feel the tenderness
of the snowwhite petals
and see a little sun
shining in every single heart
do we not see anymore
the beauty in small things
the simple joys of life
so precious, so priceless
as if God himself says
who loves my little creations
loves me

# LAST WILL

As I stepped into the sunlight
breathing in
the icy cold air
I smelt the spring coming
like little waves
in a crystal clear sky
little red robin
sang his song
trying to attract
a female to start
a new family, a new line
a little yellow crocus
just put its little head
towards the bright light
and its was like
time started a new area
hope filled my heart
maybe
a new spring
would shake this world awake
and would make people realise
that this world doesn`t need us
but we need this world
to survive

# WE WERE NOT MEANT TO BE IN A CHERRY PIE

If you and me
would be a fruit
we would be cherries
connected by a pedicel
starting our lives together
as little pink and white flowers
caressing ourselves
in the early spring sun
touching each other
our petals in the wind
as butterflies and bees
declare their love
to our pistils
then we will grow
and slowly, over weeks
turn from green to red
juicy, shiny red
enjoying the summer rains
like a shower on our delicate skin
till some child
picks and eats us.

# DAISIES ARE MY FAVOURITE

He loves me
he loves me not
he loves me
one by one
the petals fall
the wind catches them
before they reach the floor
I just sit there
with a daisy in my hand
the white petals
the golden heart
they seem to whisper
keep hoping, don't give up
one by one
the white summer snowflakes
are blown away
twirling around in the breeze
my eyes follow them
watching their dance of dreams
till the last petal falls
and I take another daisy, maybe this time.....

# LOOKING FOR...

The wind plays a game
high up in the sky
making the clouds
all go wild
here on earth
the leaves play a dangerous game
chasing each other
on the road

Nothing better to do
I stare out of the window
my mind restless
my heart far away
my eyes watch
but they see nothing
no leaves, no clouds
only the invisible wind
plays with my mind
making me see things
that could be

# I LOVE YOU, PAPA

I look at you
you try to smile
your eyes look tired
like they already gave up
your last big battle
I can see the sparkle
the little flame
that tells me
you love me
I always felt safe
when you were near
you gave me so much
all my life
and even now
I know you see
the little girl
that I once was
your life is ending
and very soon
there will be
a final
farewell

# KIENDJE

Kiendje he said and smiled
I have to go, he said
take me with you
if its only around the block
and I knew
what he meant
so we went
to the places he loved in his life
where my mum used to live
where he was born
and I saw him
saying goodbye.
To the memorial
where the soldiers were killed
and where he buried them
on that terrible day
that brought death to him
but also freedom
November 1944
and he cried and said
I haven`t been this happy
for a long time
thank you Kiendje
and when I come back
I will buy your book

thank you papa

# I EVEN LOOKED UNDER THE BED

I sit by your bed
and hold your hand
you smile at me
but your eyes
are not the eyes, I love
its your body
your voice
but the eyes are empty
you
are not at home
you talk about people
long gone
your mind must be like a puzzle
messed up
and the pieces
I should be on
are just missing
and never
will be found again

# IN MEMORY OF MY FATHER

Sharing
easy word, 7 letters
but so hard to do
for some of us
for better, for worse
happiness
we share so easy
laughing together
hugs and kisses
with good friends
some wine, some music
words flow so easy
but you always want to say more
then your lips are able to
sadness
can be harder
eating your tears
afraid somebody sees
and judges
but aren`t we all free
to decide for ourselves
when it’s time to mourn
over a lost life, a lost love
and isn`t it the biggest love
that makes us share those feelings
with family and friends
with loved ones

# THE FUNERAL

It is freezing outside
my breath makes
little white clouds
hanging around my head
and the December wind
chases them into thin air
inside
this loss makes me cold
deeper than my skin
my bones
but then
there is your hand
you told me
I am here with you
never alone, never lost
and the knowing of your touch
softly warms me
brings back
life into my body, my heart
you cannot chase away
the cold of winter
but you made
that cold, lonely feeling inside
vanish by your love

# IS THIS THE ANSWER?

You say
I sold our friendship
for a silver coin and drinks
but what is friendship
when you doubt it
what is it worth
when one has to just do
as the other feels
no turning right
no turning left
just follow that path
that you think should be followed
not being me, myself
but being how you think, I should be
so who sold
and who bought
and who lost
we both did

# HELP YOURSELF

I try to break
through a wall of ice
a glacier covered me
I can see outside
the golden sun
that tries to reach to me
but this prison
that just locked me up
it wont go away
and if I blew
it into dust
those splinters still would stay

They wounded deep
this heart of mine
covered it all with cold
they freeze and bite
and let me bleed
even if I want to be bold
the ice it burns
and will leave scars
for that I have no doubt
I fight and fight
to get out of here
I kick and push and shout

But like a wall
soundproof and huge
no one can hear me scream
all I can do
is pray and hope
that this is all a dream
that tomorrow I wake

I open my eyes
and it was all a lie
that I feel the sun
burning on my skin
and see the deep blue sky

Its is on ourselves
to safe our souls
to help turn right from wrong
to struggle and fight
and hope God might
to come and help along
Depend on yourself
and fight your fights
against demons and yourself
be proud and walk straight
let yourself never wait
you are your biggest help

# AN EMPTY SHELL

All that left
an empty shell
without the love inside
the fire gone
my feelings burned
only ashes after that night
I feel like laying
in the sand
with no heart at all
just let me lay here
don't pick me up
let me be where I did fall

Why do we need
this awful pain
this hunger never done
why do we hope
for better each time
even after love has gone
so I'll just wait
and hope the best
till a brand-new day will start
maybe some day
I will feel again
love glowing in my heart

# I AM READY

I lived through yesterday
now I am ready to face tomorrow

Today
is another story
today is sweet
but with bitter edges
april spoils me
with sunshine
and soft breezes
that are dwelling
in the green ivy
and seem to chase
sparrows and blackbirds
from a feast, a meal
devour
or be eaten yourself
I see the beauty
but also the tragedy
of life in a picture
softened by tender green

And tomorrow I will think...again

I lived through yesterday
I am ready to face tomorrow

# A FAMILY STORY

Father sits so proud
the head of the table is his
but the Mrs. of the house rules
she has the last word in this
all laws are made by her
and no one better misunderstand
a cold smile, they can get
so better behave in the end

The daughter got carried away
with distractions of all kind
and when she cannot cope
she leaves the dinner table behind
locks herself in her room
where she talks to her dolls and bear
where she writes in her diaries
and sometimes sheds a tear

The son, lost and found
tries to warm in his father's light
weighs every word, he speaks
shows now his best side
the calf, they provided for him
for his homecoming feast to hold
has been cooked and eaten for long
it was very good, I was told

And at the warm fire
the granny sits all alone
she hears their arguments
and just feels cold to the bone
she prays to God above
to take her soon from here
cause in a house without love
its not the death you should fear

# FAKE

A plastic smile
to decorate my lips
thats what I wear, you see
I got it at some store
the lady, that sold it
promised life long guarantee
she said, you won't regret
this one will never fade
it keeps by rain and shine
so now I walk straight
with a smile on my face
a smile that isn't mine

# MEMORIAL

I know, I deserve it
so put me out
with the garbage
in between
the sacks with old clothes
smelly veggies
and left overs
from last week
slices of bread
all green and slimy
a rat will sniffle at me
a dog maybe will try
to get a piece of my leg
and when that van is coming
to pick us up
all the wasted things
from your yesterday
maybe I will shed
a last tear
and get my resting place
on that huge mountain
no shield with a name
no sign saying
here lies........
maybe just
a lonely poppy
waving in the wind

# KNOCK KNOCK

Do you really think
that running away
can make it all well again
chase away the ghosts
that haunt you at night
knocking on your walls
and the noise of chains
that keeps you out of your sleep
it will haunt you
anywhere you run to
if its far away
another coast, another shore
if its mountains
or even in the deepest jungle
the ghost of yesterdays love
can only be chased away by
tomorrows sweetheart

# APRIL FOOL

She swallows all the pain
that i s eating her inside
last night, he told her
there is someone else
in my life, in my heart
there will be room for you
but just as much
as I allow there to be
the other woman
she can comfort me
with her presence
her touch of flesh

She always knew
that love means sharing
that the fear
of being left behind
will be her destiny
that breaking her heart
started the day they met
but that the love for him
will never stop growing

# DETOUR

Today
they closed the road
thats leads to my door
to my heart
for maintenance
they told me
to cut the branches
of the rose bush
to avoid me and others
from getting hurt
from the sharp thorns
so that they and me
would not bleed
but I said, he
I love it's roses, white and sweet
its like the innocence
is never far away in my life
but no, they said
and a sign was put up
stop here please
but I wish
they will open up again
real soon

# LOST

a window of hope
the hope
that keeps me going on
living
dreaming
smiling
but in my heart
I know
this hope
is so fragile
so far from reality
so far
as you are from me

# BUT WHEN DID IT MOVE?

I knock at the door
it opens, squeaking
I only see a face
old, wrinkled
a trembling hand
holding a candle
visions of wax
playing hide and seek
in my restless mind
I ask, nearly whisper
is this where love lives
and the voice answers
love doesn't live her anymore
it moved
to next door

# I WONDER

When the fire is dying
that flame of love
when the nights get chilly
and you move away
trying to avoid my touch
then my mind wonders
about days, long ago
when you couldn't
get enough
of touching me
kissing me
when our days were filled
with kisses
and I love you
when what we had
was only ours
so tell me please
when was that moment
when love moved
to next door?

# BREAKFAST

Did you know, I tried to have some
breakfast down at Tiffany's
but they sell only diamonds
and that is much too expensive for me
no toast, no juice, no little egg
boiled or fried, no chance at all
I was very disappointed
in that movie, they had a ball

I have seen some tramps lately
but they played a different song
when I asked to have breakfast
they looked at me
now don`t get me wrong
we will do that ham and egg thing
but another context you see
if you want to join us, gladly
if not.. just let it be

So I wandered a little further
and I came across a guy
he sold burgers and some dogs too
and I stopped to ask him why
people eat that here for breakfast
doughnuts and that whole fat stuff
he just grinned and counted his cash then
all the dimes and shiny quarters
and said.. that is what the people love

So I came to one conclusion
the best breakfast is with you
with the one, I love so dearly
and no matter what we do

what we eat or drink or neither
as long as I can see your eyes
we can spend all day eating breakfast
for with you its like time flies
so feed me bread and feed me butter
strawberries with cream I like best
and if we can give it a try dear
then the time will do the rest

# AROUND THE WORLD

On a slow boat to China
you taught me how to use
those chopsticks for dinner
and I was not amused
when you laughed at me trying
to get the food into my mouth
so i started using my fingers
and I said.. I can do without

On a rainy day in Georgia
when the view was almost gone
I told you all my stories
of how the war was won
you were sitting at my feet and
put your hand upon my knee
when we both discussed out loudly
how a battle of sexes should be

On a snowwhite night in Iceland
with a fire burning hot
you showed me your collection of pebbles
and told me how you got
that one there from the glacier
and that one down the sea
and I watched your eyes glowing
and knew one pebble would be me

Just take me around the world dear
and show me everything
all the wonders that surround us
all miracles, little things
the dew drop on a daffodil
a snowflake white and clear
for the biggest wonder in the world
is for me to have you near

# THIS PRECIOUS HEART

Bumblebee
you and me
in each others eyes, we see
birds and bees
christmas trees
open shores and deep blue sees
we were meant
heaven send
knowing this will never end
we will share
always fair
when I stumble, you'll be there
for my eyes
read your why's
never need to ask you twice
hear my call
see me fall
in your arms, I will have it all
sun and moon
midnight, noon
our heaven will start very soon
nights of grey
silent pray
will take us to the final day
never apart
you will guard
with your love this precious heart

# ELEMENTS

Let me be the water
that wakes up your face
in the early morning
slowly gliding
from your cheek onto your chest
and carefully dried
by the softness
of a fresh smelling towel

Let me be the wind
slowly caressing your hair
dividing it while you enjoy
the ride with open windows
the yellow engine of your truck
sings us a lullaby
and we both sing along

Let me be the moonlight
that freezes in blue
the emotions of a night
while we embrace
on a silver lighted porch
and let the silence of the night
cover us up in love

# DEATH WAKE

He watches her leave
holding her hand
so small, so cold
once
she was alive
living just for him
and now she is fighting
for every breath
for a glimpse oh her beloved
her eyes are closed
and her heart beats slow
her life
is like a flame
flickering
in the cold wind
fighting
to find fuel
desperate
to hold on
a cold wind
and the flame dies
a last breath of air
a last whisper of hope
soon she will be
a dream in his mind
like an image
in the dust of time
a fading picture
of a lost love
and the tears
on his rippling cheek
will drip on the roses
he will put on her little grave
every day
from now on

# PRICELESS

I hold a treasure
very close to me
I don't have to hide it
from someone seeing it, you see
It's not made of silver
it's not made of gold
but to it is priceless
to have and to hold

No diamonds that sparkle
no pearls grown in the sea
but warmth and tenderness
are waiting for me
Yes, it can be stolen
and God knows, I pray
that I can hold it for always
forever and a day

But the one who will take it
will love it like I do
will respect and care for it
will now make it feel blue
then I don't have to worry
that my treasure will fade
and that true love, like I feel it
will be betrayed

Yes, I have a treasure
and I don't want to part
cause my only richness
is...... your heart

# MY SMILES ARE FOR FREE

My words
they only cost your time
the time you have
to invest in them
my words
they come in whispers
telling of love
sometimes
it seems unsure
but in my heart
solid as a rock
that this is so right
no other way
no looking back
whispering in your ear
just takes you
to make some time
for me
my smiles
they are for free

# YELLOW ROSES

Thorns
under my skin
grown in
pain when I touch
I look
but cannot see
who is guilty
of this pain
a rosebush
with a scent so sweet
can cause
so much pain
barely touch it
and it attacks you
with thorns
sharp as knives
a price you pay
for smelling
admiring it's wonders
Thorns under my skin
grown in
pain when I think of you
they must have gone
all the way
to my vulnerable heart
who is guilty
not us
for falling in love
an attack, we didn't expect
to hit so hard, so deep
sweet pain
is the price we pay
for what one day
will be ours

# FOREVER

The song takes me
by my trembling hand
and takes me
to that special place
I have for you
deep in a corner of my heart
there is a candle
forever burning
softly flickering
in a gentle summer breeze
where high up a small kite
dances the dance of love
with all the colours
of a rainbow
a book lies there
with all the poems i wrote for you
and every time
when my heart
feels heavy with sadness
thats where
my sanctuary will be
a place, only for you and me
to have and to hold
enough love
to last a lifetime

# LIGHTHOUSE

When my sea is rough
when lightning flogs the skies
you are the light
in my harbour
to safety - to the shore

When the fog is heavy
when I am lost and
my sight goes dim
you are the light
in my harbour
you guide me
to a place to rest

When the storm fights me
when the waves threaten to devour me
you are the light
in my harbour
you save me
guide me home

But darling
don't forget to change the bulb now and then

# I WISH I WAS A CLOUD SOMETIMES

Clouds never sleep
they drift away
where ever the winds
wants them to
they cannot have dreams
desires
they just obey
to higher powers
they cannot be hurt
torn apart
they just sail on
and watch the world
and at the end
all thats left is
water

# DEDICATED

How was your day, my love
you ask with a tender smile
wonderful as ever
I reply with a sigh
through the window
I see this bright star
twinkling in the velvet dark
you light some candles
and the sweet smell
of cinnamon fills the room
soft music plays
and the pillows look inviting
I close my eyes
soon sweet dreams
will fill my tired mind
in my neck, I feel
soft lips kissing me
and they seem to whisper
what a perfect ending
to a perfect day

# IF

If I was going to be blind
I would still remember your face
from all the times
that my fingers wondered
across your cheek
caressing and feeling your soft skin

If I was going to be deaf
I would still hear your voice
whispering in my ear
sweet words of love
and your music I hear in me

If I was going to lose my touch
my fingertips would still remember
the curves of your body
the strength of your muscles
your arms holding me

If I was going to lose my smell
my nose would still remember
the sweet scent of your skin
the pearls of sweat after a night of loving
the freshness that water brings to your body

If I was going to lose my taste
my lips, my tongue would still remember
the taste of your mouth
your hot kisses in the night

If I was going to lose all my senses
I would never stop
loving your body, your soul
with all my heart

I would give up
my eyes, ears, touch, smell and taste
but my heart will never give up you

# MESSAGE IN A BOTTLE

The silence
of your voice
screams in my head
I need you
but you are so far
and all I can do
is try to be here for you
when the longing
reaches the borders
that you have set
for yourself.

# BROWNIES AND A DIET COKE

I open my eyes
and see you lying next to me
my fingers touch
your lips
you smile and reach out
with closed eyes
you pull me close
my body is touching yours
I feel your breath
on my cheeks
you sigh, I sigh
sunbeams
drawing lines on the wall
I close my eyes again
I love Sunday mornings

# VISIONS OF WAX

The candle on the table
is flickering in the dark
the flame is restless
your face close to mine
your eyes telling me
how much you care
my tears
they cause the light
to break
in a million colors
a million rainbows
is it only my imagination
is it an invisible wind
is it your breath
suddenly
the flame dies
darkness
the end

# ONE DAY

I would give a thousand lives
just for one with you
for even one day, one night
to taste the forever true
because looking in your eyes
I see the love
thats ancient, now and new

# AT LAST

I count the daisies
that lie shattered on the floor
I sigh and then giggle
this last one in my hand
finally told me
what I was waiting for
as the last petal fell
it said, he loves me
and so I will take
the golden heart
and sent it to you
as a gift from me
to make you smile
to tell you
I love you too

# OUR WORDS

Everything
that ever exists
will turn to dust
sooner or later
buildings
people created
to last for centuries
our bodies, our bones
your beloved face
my smile
but there will always be
songs, words
forgotten in time maybe
but never in the soul
and some day
some one, somewhere
will discover them
will think they are new
and will never know
what they already meant
to you and me

# PILLOW TALK

If this bed could talk
If the sheets could tell their story
It would mention
The passion, we share
The hot kisses
The caressing
The touch of skin to skin
The sounds, the whispering
And what I would hear most
Is us saying
I love you